That's Terrible 2

A Cringeworthy Collection of 1001

~~Really Bad~~ *Even Worse* Jokes!

By

Gary Rowley

For the UK & Ireland Salesforce, wrap around, and everyone at Hardy & Greys

Back by popular demand: another rib-tickling collection of 1001 original jokes and one-liners - only this time *even worse!* Like its hugely entertaining big sister, this addictive little gem will have you in stitches from the word go. Plumbed once more from the innermost depths and far-out corridors of an extremely vivid imagination, it will appeal to kids and grandmas, whilst still supplying sufficient ammunition to torment your mates into submission. Just like the first time, all you need to do to become immersed in this barrage of off-the-wall buffoonery is find a quiet spot somewhere then slowly turn the page...

Enjoy!

ET's been caught shoplifting. I always said he was light fingered.

Animal rights activists are currently camped outside United's training ground after it was announced Wayne Rooney had injured a calf.

I staggered out of the pub and straight into a fracas with a rag and bone man. I was charged with junk and disorderly.

The wife asked if I fancied a trip to the Arctic Circle. I said, sounds cool.

I took my car back to the garage. I said, every time it rains, I get this awful hissing noise. The mechanic said, I wouldn't worry too much. It's probably just the windscreen vipers.

Ghosts: they need to get a life.

I bought an imitation American motorcycle. It was a Hardly Davidson.

My job at the glue factory, I've told them to stick it.

I went in HMV. I said, what do you think to the Pet Shop Boys? The assistant said, they've a good selection of dog biscuits but the prices are a bit steep.

Tardis for sale. No time wasters.

I took my new DAB radio back to the shop. I said, the volume button is stuck on low and I don't know what to do. He said, try playing it by ear.

The cat o' nine tails I inherited: I've flogged it.

I may have failed sniper school. But at least I gave it my best shot.

Crossing this river, I noticed dozens of fancy chocolates, floating gently downstream. It was a bridge over truffled water.

I'm salaried in raisins. I have them paid straight into my currant account.

Chiropodists: they don't half earn their corn.

I opened this shop, selling budgies. They're flying out of the door.

When I was in the army, I spent three months drinking strong beer. I was on special hops.

I told the doctor I was concerned about my weight. He said, it looks like you've got an over active...Thyroid gland, I interrupted? He said, no, knife and fork!

I fell in love with a female refuse collector. Then she dumped me.

My daughter has a poster of this emaciated pop star above her bed. It's Ribbie Williams.

I bought a house in Brazil. I must have been nuts.

That new chick flick was a bit disappointing. It was all about a hen, playing Subbuteo.

I think my dad's fantastic. I think my little boy's fantastic as well. Like father, like son.

Philadelphia PA: it's me. I'm personal assistant to a tub of soft cheese.

I was invited to a fancy dress party and there was this bloke with a football pools coupon, pinned to his torso. He'd come as a chest of draws.

Glossy magazines: I've got a few issues.

I love pub food. In actual fact, I might have a Royal Oak sandwich for tea.

Last night: I remember it like it was yesterday.

I said, doctor, I keep thinking I'm a giant mollusc. I felt a lot better once he'd had a word in my shell-like.

Newsflash: Man arrested for armed robbery at the trifle factory has been remanded in custardy.

I said, doctor, I keep thinking I'm Robert the Bruce. He said, great Scot!

My job at the Kodak factory: it was hard graft, but the camera-arderie was fantastic.

I saw a sign saying, Norman church. When I got there, it was some bloke called Norm on St Mary's roof, replacing broken tiles.

Parcel van for sale. Can deliver.

I saw a sign saying, mud on road. When I turned the corner, it was a seventies' glam rock band, singing a song called Tiger Feet.

Bank robbers: they're pinching a living.

I was a bit surprised to learn my sister was going out with a boxer. I was even more surprised to discover it was a big, brown dog with a flat nose and pointed ears.

People mock when I tell them I used to be a farmer. I don't know why. I was outstanding in my field.

I popped in the Chinese, and there was this pink crustacean, running amok. It was prawn crackers.

The boss insisted I took a lieu day. So I spent eight hours on the pot, reading the paper.

I discovered an almanac, containing next season's football results. Talk about a know-win situation.

I went for a swim and was immediately surrounded by ten thousand goats, all singing Caribbean Queen. It was the Billy Ocean.

People taking a dip in the sea off Great Yarmouth today were mysteriously attacked then devoured by dolphins, with survivors airlifted to a nearby campsite. The PM has expressed his heartfelt condolences, to all in tents and porpoises.

I'd enrol for embroidery class...if I wasn't so darn busy.

This sign on the motorway said, pedestrians in road, slow. Let me tell you this: they soon got a sprint on when they saw me coming towards them at a hundred miles per hour.

I put Newsnight on and there was this silhouetted character, spouting on about the economy. I think it was the shadow chancellor.

Dozens of twelve bores were gathered outside the church, showering confetti upon a twelve bore in a smart suit and another in a bridal gown. I thought, whey hey, a shotgun wedding.

I was walking through Westminster and saw this government minister, beating up an electric meter. I thought, that's an abuse of power.

My gearbox went. Or at least I thought it was my gearbox until I was rudely informed it was the camshaft. I said to the mechanic, alright, calm down: I'm entitled to my pinion, aren't I?

I drove over the Forth Road Bridge. But I couldn't see anything of the other three.

Sixties pop icon Sandie Shaw. She's just bought a house on Beachy Head.

I was making Tom Yam Goong when my neighbour came round and asked if I could give him a lift with a grand piano. I said, I'd love to, but unfortunately my hands are Thaied.

Hampton Court: it's a maze in, innit?

I followed signs for Newark. When I got there, it was pouring rain and there was this bloke, putting the finishing touches to his new boat, while the animals were entering two by two.

As a pack of rabid wolves crested the horizon, the first shepherd said to the second shepherd, let's get the flock out of here.

I enquired about holidays to Rumania. I said, I need to Buch-a-rest.

My cross-eyed girlfriend: I'm sure she's seeing someone else.

I lost my job this morning. I popped out for a sandwich and couldn't find my way back to the industrial estate.

I was on this motorway, where the hard shoulder was made from lengths of neatly-folded, hand-stitched cloth. I learned later it was the Hem 1.

There was a big fight this morning at the bakery. Police have described the incident as unsavoury.

There was another fight later in the cafe, but nothing like as serious. Police said it was no more than a storm in a teacup.

I asked this bloke what kind of car he drove. He purred then said, Joe.

What will the weather be like on the 5th of November? It's the burning question.

I applied for a full time course at college. When I got there, it was a classroom full of trainee referees, practising blowing whistles.

My friend's crazy about pavements. I've told him he needs to kerb his enthusiasm.

I've just found out my wife isn't a figment of my imagination, after all. How Sue-real.

Sentry duty: I can't stand it.

I bumped into Crippen in the pub. I said, what's your poison?

The day of reckoning has finally arrived. My maths exam is at two o'clock.

I was in a pub in Portsmouth when this group of newspaper reporters came in and started dragging blokes off to join the navy. I thought, ooh look, a press gang.

Every morning at seven, I get up and do the Cha-cha-cha. I make three cups of tea.

When I leave for work, my cereals wave me bye-bye: they're Cheerios.

I'm on a downward spiral. I'm addicted to helter skelters.

I put Singapore down as deposit on my new car. It was port exchange.

Julia Roberts has made a follow up to nineties classic, Sleeping with the Enemy, in which she's being hunted by an obsessive music journalist. Released next week, it's called, Sleeping with the NME.

I went in this sports shop and there were dozens of pairs of shoes, enjoying a work-out. I thought, ooh look, trainers.

My girlfriend soon livens up when the sun comes out. Her name is Sarah...Sarah Tonin.

I was watching that 1980s Irene Cara film last night, the one about teenagers in a New York dance school, but the tele packed in after quarter of an hour. Oh well, I suppose I can always say I've have had my fifteen minutes of Fame.

This bloke kept trying to sell me a long, wooden platform, stretching out to sea. I didn't buy it. I refused to give in to pier pressure.

I said, half a pound of bacon, please. She said, smoked? I said, packed it in six weeks ago...now, half a pound of bacon, please.

The supervisor's vacancy at the chicken factory, I'm well down the pecking order.

I booked a spa evening. I got knocked out in the first round.

It's just been announced that, with regret, the West Midlands Glue Company is now insolvent.

I found an ear in the pub. This bloke, missing an ear, came up to me and said, I thought that was mine at first, but it can't be. I said, why not? He said, mine had a fag behind it.

My seventies Ford: I fell in love with her the night we met. I thought, Cor, Tina!

I ran a mile when I encountered this vicious, dog-like creature, dressed up as Freddy Krueger. I think it was a wolf in creep's clothing.

My wife, the traffic warden: don't trouble yourself, she's in fine fettle.

I went in Curry's and this salesman sold me an interest free TV. He wasn't kidding. I've never seen such a load of twaddle in my life.

That bloke behind the wheel of the number 22 bus: he drives me round the bend.

I rule the world. I'm a cartographer.

Wages at the ketchup factory: tax is deducted at sauce.

I've just bought a twenty foot horse. I'll let you know how I get on.

My PC developed a virus: the doctor prescribed amoxicillin.

I threw this party. My dog chased it.

There's this Red Indian tribe that takes its name from its chief, the one who loves hip-hop music and never stops laughing. It's A Rapper Ho.

There's another tribe that gets its name from the local Sherriff's bashful daughter. It's Shy Anne.

And another named after my Aunt Susan (abbreviated).

When I was looking for a baby sitter, I gave the job to a Native American. I was told to hire-Watha.

A cowboy went online: Yahoo!

I went in the kitchen, and the lettuce, cucumber, onion and tomato were all dancing away to Thin Lizzy songs. It's the last time I'll be buying rock it salad.

Redundancies are on the cards at the Chinese food blender factory. Two hundred jobs are at whisk.

I went to bed but forgot to turn the landing light off. When I got up, there was a Boeing 747 parked outside my door.

Big job on tonight: washing an elephant down.

I rang this number and the phone display read, engaged. I looked at my new fiancé and thought, aah, what a lovely touch...

United took to the field in muddy shirts and shorts. Alex Ferguson had named an unchanged team.

I used to be a lumberjack. Then I was axed.

My composting company has fallen upon hard times. I'll be out of business if I don't find a way to stop the rot.

I went in this army canteen. What a mess.

Guess who I bumped into on my way to the opticians? Everybody I saw.

I was leading the world wind turbine self-assembly championships by a mile. Then I blew it.

I put Blind Date on but it's the last time. It was all about pieces of dried fruit, learning to read Braille.

Monday morning stubble: it's rough going.

I was mucking out at the farm when this bloke came up and asked if he could snog a horse. I told him to kiss my ass.

My troubled tree surgeon's business: I've ordered a root and branch review.

I went on an Arctic cruise and saw this singing ice floe, giving a hearty rendition of Lady in Red. It was Chris de Berg.

I've just seen a bloke with the Red Baron, sticking out of his jumper. Talk about an ace up his sleeve.

My dad says I have his genes. Don't make me laugh. They're two sizes too big, for a start, and torn at the seam from when he bent over, digging the back garden...

I've just done seventeen marathons in a week: you know, those nut-filled chocolate bars that are now called Snickers.

Every time I visit the supermarket, there's a complete aisle filled with bottles labelled, still water. Of course it is! What are they hoping for? To arrive one morning and discover it's turned into red wine?

I bought a prehistoric skull for a fiver. It was a no-brainer.

Rats: they breed like rabbits.

I've just seen this bloke, stapling his head. I think he was pinning his ears back.

It was the most traumatic experience of my life when I was locked overnight in the sausage factory. Honestly, I was climbing the Walls.

I've just seen this bloke, practising his golf swing in the rear of a car, whilst hurtling down the motorway at one hundred miles per hour. He was obviously a back seat driver.

A friend of mine went to Lancashire and bought a lorry made from fresh flowers. It was a Leyland Daf.

I've broken up with my hairdresser girlfriend. We tried and tried but found we just couldn't gel.

Did you see the big film last night, the one about an uprising aboard an ocean going bar of chocolate: it was Mutiny on the Bounty.

I asked the wife what she was doing, smearing strawberry jam over the electrical points. She said she was conserving energy.

My plumbing business: it's going down the pan.

I've just been fleeced at pontoon by that bloke who directed the Death Wish trilogy. I thought, typical: Winner takes all.

Short tongued, inner city women: they're an urban myth.

I shouted beneath the bathroom door, what's the capital of England? This gruff voice replied, Helsinki. It was the thick bleach.

Peking duck: it's watching you.

I'm in court tomorrow, charged with breaking into the library. Word on the street is they'll throw the book at me.

I was involved in a collision with an Elvis impersonator. He was all shook up.

Granny Smith: she's the apple of my eye.

I ordered korma, biryani then vindaloo, but was rudely informed they were out of the lot. That's the last Indian I'll be ordering at Curry's.

I said, doctor, people are spreading it round that I have chronic inflammation of the knee joints. He said, it sounds like a classic case of rumour-toid-arthritis.

My hairdressing job isn't the best paid. But at least I have plenty of fringe benefits.

I used to drive a Lada. It was OK, but tins of beans kept falling on my head.

A basketball player just read me a fairy tale. Talk about a tall story.

I can't say I thought much of the new A-Team movie. If you ask me, it was all about Face.

Did you hear about the cannibal that was caught poaching?

I said, doctor, I keep getting ringing in my ears. He said, have you tried answering it?

A shipment of false moustaches has gone missing from the local joke shop. The manager said they disappeared right from under his nose.

I took my laptop abroad, hit the return key and finished up back at Manchester Airport.

I've just been made redundant from the fishmongers: gutted doesn't come into it.

My mate said, how do you fancy going to a concert of intricate, propulsive rhythms, with polyphonic ensemble, plus improvisatory, virtuosic solos, melodic freedom, and a harmonic idiom ranging from simple diatonicism through chromaticism to atonality? I said, nah, I can't be doing with all that jazz.

I submitted a passport application form. I got it in a headlock and it tapped out.

Doctor Who's wife is adamant their recent split is only temporary. She was heard to say, he'll take me back in time.

I could tell you a joke about herbs and fish, but it's hardly the thyme or plaice.

Tanning salons: it's like being in the Bronze Age.

I went to the footie. When the visitors scored, this dog did a triple salco down the terrace then hopped back up on its hind legs. I said to the owner, what's it do when City score? He said, don't ask me: I've only had it six years.

Twenty-seven women called Elizabeth lined up for a race. All Bets are off...

I named my new dog after a famous warrior from Greek mythology. You may have heard me training him in the park: Achilles, heel.

I saw the complete works of Dickens, walking down the street in trousers six inch too long. Next day, I saw them again and the trousers fitted perfectly. I thought, that's a turn up for the books.

Every time my mate gets arrested, he blames me. I'll swing for him one of these days.

I started work at the rubber factory. My first pay cheque bounced.

It's just been on the news that several people have been arrested after a consignment of luggage went missing from Manchester Airport. The case is ongoing.

I got a phone call from my friend, whooping with delight from his hospital bed. I said, what's up? He said, they're naming this weird disease after me.

Howard Webb: he's been nominated for the Booker Prize.

I was a bit disappointed with new pop sensations, the Dalmatians: they only did two spots.

I don't reckon much to that paint balling lark. I spent the entire day screaming my head off at two litre tins of pink emulsion.

The boss paid me a thousand pounds to peel twenty bags of onions. I was crying all the way to the bank.

I finally found my perfect match. It's slim, two inches long, and has a pink, phosphorous head.

My doctor recommended film-coated tablets. So I got the hammer out, smashed up a Pretty Woman DVD, glued the lot together, and then washed it down with a bottle of Lucozade.

I've just seen a flying Beatle. It was Paul McCartney with wings.

007: he won't take Doctor No for an answer.

Did you know that James Bond has a brother called Brooke, who works in a tea bag factory?

I used to be a stunt-double-come-handyman on the set of Goldfinger: I was the Odd Job man.

007 glue. It bonds in seconds.

I'm worried I'm eating too much junk food. I had Chinese ship sandwiches for tea again today, third time this week.

Ladies of the night: they're bonkers.

I went to the doctors, and there was this syringe, running amok in the waiting room. I thought, ooh look, a hyper-dermic-needle.

I jumped on this estate agent's toes. He said, what was all that about? I said, it was my stamp duty.

My hand-gliding business: it never really got off the ground.

I couldn't believe it when my wife threw my Aretha Franklin collection on the bonfire. Honestly, it was soul destroying.

My best friend, all he does is laze around in his favourite armchair, boring people stupid all day. That said, I'm always glad to hear his dull-sit tones.

I went scuba diving and was robbed by a fish with a machine gun. I learned later it was the Codfather.

I'm all for a fairer Britain. I think blonde hair should be made compulsory.

The wife went mad when I fetched tennis shoes instead of nappies. I could have sworn she said pumpers.

I ordered a replica of the Flying Scotsman on line. I thought I'd got a bargain: what I hadn't reckoned upon was the carriage.

Rolling roadblocks: if you see one coming, dive for cover.

I don't subscribe to all this recession talk. It's boom time at the firm where I work. You may have heard of us: we're the Sheffield Cannon and Hand Grenade Company.

All the tills at the supermarket were manned by skeletons: they were clearly down to the bare bones.

I saw thousands of brooms, speeding around in motor cars. It was obviously the brush hour.

Those nice people at the Magaluf Snorkelling Company: they're struggling to keep their heads above water.

I've got form. I stole a bench out of the park.

There was a big fight at the circus. This clown walloped a sword swallower then went straight for the juggler.

I fancy becoming an Eskimo fisherman. But I know it's never going to harpoon.

I stole a calendar. I got twelve months.

I refused to answer question ten in last night's pub quiz: who masterminded the infamous 1987 Brink's-Mat robbery? I knew who it was: but I'm not a grass.

My builder hit me a five grand bill for my new roof. I put it on the slate.

I was elected for parliament when the opposition candidate was buried alive by falling rocks. I won by a landslide.

I've fallen upon hard Times. I went walking in the snow and tripped over a frozen newspaper.

Leadless pencils: I can't see any point in them?

I went to Disney World and got into an argument with this bloke in a furry rodent costume. When he raised his hands in submission, I said, what are you? Man or mouse?

My wife thinks my infatuation with Wi-Fi is getting out of hand. She says I'm absolutely hub-sessed.

I own a house in Norway, overlooking the fjords. I have to say they have some spectacular Mondeo offers this month.

When my book, A History of Slapstick, went straight to the top of the bestsellers chart, I immediately started work on the follow up. I couldn't see any point resting on my Laurels.

Did you know the capital of Libya is Tripoli, and that it was named after an infamous Laurel and Hardy tour, when some local wag made a name for himself by deliberately tripping Ollie?

I come from a broken home. All the windows are smashed and the electricity doesn't work.

My guest appearance for the dentists' footie team went down a treat. I bagged a brace.

I went to a bees' nightclub. The place was buzzing.

First day in the Paras and I got the runs. I didn't let it stop me, though: I hit the ground running.

I asked this waiter for a glass of cool pop. He fetched dandelion and burdock in sunglasses and a snazzy Hawaiian shirt.

The truth's out. It had a scrap with false and took one on the chin in round two.

I won a chicken in a raffle. I can't believe my cluck.

My driving instructor told me to take the next left. I thought, that's not right.

I've just heard the apprentice puppeteer's job I went for is mine if I want it. I just hope they're not stringing me along.

I've just seen a biro, dealing drugs. I thought, ooh look, a pen pusher.

Kernel Tom Parker: what a nut.

I went to a funfair without any rides: it was no thrills.

I've just started work as a nanny. I go to work in a furry goat suit.

My darling mother, bless her heart, she's only three foot tall. Little wonder she's worried by proposals for a mini-Mum price on alcohol.

I was on the motorway and saw these blokes, having a tug of war with a piece of elasticated tarmac. It must have been a stretch of road.

After twenty-seven years at the bakery, I've suddenly decided I hate my job. I think I must be having a mid-loaf crisis.

I went to the police station and was greeted by a wooden table in a pointed helmet. It was the desk sergeant.

This female sheep threatened to kick my head in. I said, that's big of ewe.

I went to the museum and saw this curator, mistreating a dinosaur skeleton. Talk about bad to the bone.

This sign said, danger, elderly people. No kidding? I slowed down and one of them threw a brick through my window.

I was in Geneva when this huge fleet of limousines drove past. It was a Swiss cortege.

When I was in Tibet, there was this important religious bloke doing the rounds, dressed in a black and white spotted suit, and barking like a dog. It was the Dally Lama.

I arrived home to find the wife, wallpapering my PC. I don't think she quite got the gist when I told her to cut and paste.

Long John Silver: he was a leg end in his own lifetime.

I wish I'd never bought that desk fan. All it does all day is sing, we all love desk and desk, and desk, desk and desk, and desk and desk, and desk, and desk and desk, we all flipping love desk...

That Shakespearean night at the local theatre: a big fight broke out when a bloke in row three developed an irritating tickle. If you ask me, it was much ado about coughing.

When I was at school, I had my backside tanned. It was a really eye-catching, soft brown colour.

I was visiting Warsaw, when this bloke came up to me and said, dit, dit, dot, dit, dot, dot, dit, dit, dot. I thought, whey hey, a telegraph Pole.

I was watching the DNA results on Jeremy Kyle: it was 2-1 to the mother.

The teacher said, I want you to write a sentence using the words narrative, meaning tale, and extinguish, meaning to put out. So I wrote, when the cat started meowing, I picked it up by its tale and extinguished it.

If anyone would like to read my award-winning essay on the subject of my pet cat, here it is: I let Tiddles out last night. When it was time to come in, I went to the door and shouted, here, puss, puss, puss, puss. Here, puss, puss, puss, puss....

I didn't know where to start with my essay on dead flies. So I looked on the web.

There was this football agent in the bank with Steven Gerrard on his head. I think he was doing a balance transfer.

I was on my way into the big cats enclosure at Chester zoo when a sign fell off the wall, knocking this bloke unconscious. Subsequent investigations revealed it was the I of the tiger.

I've just formed a splinter group: it's an association for people who get pieces of wood lodged down the back of their nails.

My mate collects hand woven, wickerwork shopping hampers. If you ask me, he's a right basket case.

I was driving down this road in Germany, and was shocked to find it covered with bales of hay and random farm animals. Then I realised: I was on the auto barn.

If pigs could fly, would the price of bacon go up?

I've just seen this waste paper basket, performing stunts on a motorbike. I thought, whey hey, a wheelie bin.

My maths teacher was crying her eyes out. I said, what's wrong? She said, two-plus-two equals five.

I went to see the Hungarian GP. Nothing against people from Budapest, of course, it was just that all the other doctors were booked up.

This cowboy asked me to lend him a fiver. I think it was Skint Eastwood.

I've just started higher education. My new school is at the top of Mount Everest.

Someone asked me what that minty, gel-like stuff was called, the stuff that provides relief from mouth ulcers. I said, just hang on a sec' and I'll tell you. It's on the tip of my tongue.

I was guest of honour at a cannibal's birthday party. We played silly games and cut the cake: then they toasted me.

I'm buying this repossessed house in America. It's in some place called Amityville.

John Smith: talk about bitter.

I decided to dig a trench round the edge of this field. Then I ditched the idea.

My deep sea diving business: it's sinking fast.

I nearly got knocked down by a snow plough. Watch where you're going, I yelled, through gritted teeth.

People in Rotherham can be a bit grumpy. If I were you, I wouldn't bother 'em.

I've own a pig in a pen. How it got there is anyone's guess, but at least it still seems to be writing OK.

This sign said, boarding kennels. When I got there, it was lots of dog kennels, showing off on skateboards,

I saw a tribe of Red Indians, camped out on the motorway. They were on the central reservation.

A toilet seat has been stolen from Lincoln police station. The local constabulary admit they have nothing to go on.

I came across this hand-written note, pinned to a tree in the cemetery. It said, fancy going halves to buy a colony of blood-sucking Desmodus rotundus? Just bat the idea around then let me know...signed, Van Helsing.

Doctor Hourihane told me to lie on the couch. So I made myself comfy and said, I'm a multi-millionaire, seeing Miss World, and I arrived here today by helicopter.

I was in the Chinese. Someone shouted, duck. Next thing, I was knocked unconscious by a flying chicken.

My car was overheating, so I took it back to the garage. I said, you should have seen it last night: it had fish, chips, mushy peas and three chocolate éclairs.

I shot a judge. It was an honour killing.

My big interview tomorrow, the one at the Winnie the Pooh factory: I'll need to teddy my nerves.

I love Polos. But I couldn't eat a hole one.

This bloke asked me for a lift. So I said, you're a good looking guy, oozing with charisma, and you ought to go far.

I arrived home to find the wife coppering up and crying her eyes out. I said, what's the matter? She said, I'm going through the change.

Bet you didn't know I had a police record: it's Walking on the Moon.

I took the back off my PC and this component biffed me on the nose. It was the hard drive.

U-bends: I can't get my head round them.

I work in a dictionary colliery. It's a mine of information.

I always like to keep my powder dry. If you ever visit my bathroom, check out my joke-telling talc's new material.

That joke about amnesia...how does it go?

I stopped off at the jet wash and got stuck in a queue behind a squadron of RAF Tornado GR4's.

There was a job going at Kwik Fit. Tyres and exhausts, the advert said. I thought, yeah, right, and went for this bed tester's vacancy instead.

I gave up my job as a candle stick maker. I was all burned out.

My DIY attempt in the pantry was an absolute disaster. I'm just trying not to beat my shelf up about it.

I really fancied pancakes for tea. The wife said she didn't give a toss.

When my bouncer mate called in sick, I agreed to fill in for him.

I stopped and asked this bloke for directions. He told me where to go.

Apparently this British General once lost a battle in a scrap yard: it was the battle of car tomb.

I phoned the doctors. I said, I think I've got measles. He said, don't do anything rash.

I went deep sea diving and saw this barnacle-covered vessel, shaking like a leaf. It was a nervous wreck.

There was this clamp in the woodworking shop, reciting Keats. I thought, whey hey, vice versa.

I was waiting for my prescription when the floor began to shake. I couldn't believe it: I was quaking in my Boots.

My new girlfriend, Paige, reads a dozen books a day. Her surname is Turner.

I was in the travel agents when John Travolta came in and booked a holiday to Greece.

My sailboat company, I'm thinking of floating it...

I went shopping for hair clippers. I said, where's the Braun section, mate? He said, weightlifting equipment is on the second floor, sir.

It's true what they say about beauty only being skin deep. I used to go out with this dermatologist and she was absolutely obnoxious.

I said, doctor, every time I practise my hula-hula, I get this awful tickling sensation at the back of my throat. He said, you've got hooping cough.

What do a frog and a rhinoceros have in common? Neither can tune an electric guitar.

I asked this architect when he was getting married. He said, no plans.

This sign on the motorway said, shed load. I complained to the Highways Agency when I got home. I said, there wasn't a shed in sight. In actual fact, it was a consignment of washing machines.

I went in this pub and it stank of burning hair. It was full of singe drinkers.

My job at the dilute orange plant: I find it hard to concentrate.

I called out a mobile tyre fitter and an IPhone 5 turned up with a monkey wrench.

It took me two days to complete three courses: York, Aintree and Kempton Park.

I hate Japanese aeroplanes. I've got Zero tolerance.

This bloke asked me if he could pay by cheque. I said, of course, and Josef from Prague came in and settled the bill.

I got a lift engineer's job but phoned in sick on my first day. I said, I think I'm coming down with something.

Canary for sale. Going for a song.

I went to France and came home with a leg cocooned in water mixed with calcium sulphate. It was plaster of Paris.

Did you hear about the footballer who thumped this sixties coin? He turned on a sixpence.

I was frogmarched out of this pub yesterday. The bouncer's name was Kermit.

The bloke across the street, trying to start that vintage car with a metal handle: what a crank.

I saw this armoured vehicle, scratching its turret, while sucking on a pencil. I thought, whey hey, a think tank.

Hannibal Lecter: he's making a right killing.

How do you know when you've got Hannibal Lecter in bed with you? He's got HL embroidered on his pyjamas.

I bumped into Hannibal Lecter last night and he didn't look in a good mood. In fact, he had a right face on him.

Hannibal Lecter remarked of his latest victim: I ate his guts.

I make my living buying old wells then selling them on for profit: I'm a hole-saler.

My mate thinks mushrooms are absolutely hilarious. Personally, I can't see the fungi side.

I'm really flush at the moment. I've got sixteen toilets in my spare bedroom.

I work at the docks. I sweep the surgery every morning at seven.

My boarding kennels business: it's going to the dogs.

I used to be top salesman at the Ford garage. Then I lost my Focus.

The till broke in the bakery. I said to the assistant, use your loaf.

I was in the trenches when someone shouted, incoming! Next thing, I was hit on the head by a flying pub.

That fence erector's job I applied for: I've been offered the post.

I took my new laptop back to PC World. I said, I'm struggling to get to grips with the technology. I feel ever so stupid. The assistant said, well you shouldn't do, sir. It's hardly your fault if you're a factually unencumbered, knowledge-based non-possessor now, is it...?

There was this bloke in the pub, swigging beer while enjoying a donkey ride. He was having a drink on his mate.

I went down the pub and it was filled with greasy long-hairs, smoking joints and singing peace songs. It was hippy hour.

When Lucifer came in the chippie, Mr Burgin grabbed him by the scruff of the neck and dumped him straight in the deep fat fryer. I said, batter the devil you know?

I saw a sign saying, Jesus loves you. The wife said it was the law of averages.

Bob Tanner's my best mate. I don't care if he hasn't got a penny to his name.

I said to this fishmonger, I can hear meowing. He said, new line: cat fish.

This oyster wouldn't let a shrimp have a go on its pogo stick. I said, don't be so shellfish.

I saw a sign for Wakefield. A few miles further on, there was a car pulled up on the hard shoulder, and this bloke, shaking this field, trying to wake it up.

There was one charity-runner dressed as a chicken and another dressed as an egg, neck and neck in the home stretch of the Great North Run. I thought, hmmm, now this is going to be interesting...

I asked a female street cleaner out on a date. She gave me the brush off.

When the weather forecast said gales, the last thing I expected was to find a footballer called Clichy, and a Coronation Street resident named McIntyre, blowing down the street.

I considered holidaying in India. But now it's a no Goa.

The cartoonists' club challenged the caricature society to a game of football. It was a draw.

I've just seen this bloke, walking down the street with his coat on fire. I think it was a blazer.

People say I'm half baked. What's it got to do with them if I sleep in an oven?

I used to be a Venos salesman, paid on commission. I didn't do too badly, though: there was generally a few bob in the coughers.

If at first you don't succeed, I probably wouldn't have a go at bungee jumping.

I've just discovered I'm a figment of someone's imagination. I can't believe it. In actual fact, I'm made up.

This bloke in the hotel said, there's an escaped prisoner coming down in the lift. I said, don't be so condescending.

I've just found out my windows were decorated for gallantry during the war: they're UP-VC.

It took me two hours to hail a cab. Talk about living the hoy life.

I saw a frog, illegally parked. It got toad away.

That Titanic film is a right load of twaddle. Did you see the colour of the sky when Jack and Rose were standing on the bow of the ship? Everyone knows the world was still in black and white back in 1912.

I came out of the polling station and there were all these people, bobbing along on a current of air. They must have been floating voters.

The Boston Strangler: he needs to get a grip.

I was walking past the smurf factory when the Olympic sprint champion appeared in the yard and began running, as fast as his legs would carry him. Talk about a Bolt out of the blue.

Parasite? Is it online support for ex-airborne troops?

I entrede a spede tipyng centost adn wno wtih sxi hendrud wrods purr munite.

This jobsworth turned me away from the dumpit site. I said, it's your land Phil.

We went looking at prams yesterday but didn't part with any money. It was just a dummy run.

I've just been mugged by a marauding gang of delinquent jewellery. I'll get my own back, though: I know who the ring leader is.

This advert said, hairdryer sets, half price, larger Boots only. I thought, that's no good to me: I'm only a seven.

I asked the bloke at the fruit and veg' shop if he fancied coming to Barbados with me. He said, what, on my celery?

My pal was adamant he was having the top bed. I said, I wouldn't bunk on it.

I always request my Big Macs burned to a cinder. I've got ash burgers syndrome.

Frog spawn: is it cheeky pictures of Miss Piggy?

I've just seen this Star Wars villain, being dragged out of a black-cab by officers from Her Majesty's Revenue and Customs. I thought, ooh look, a taxi-Vader.

There's this bloke on our estate, who goes round dropping milk off at houses at silly o'clock every morning. I'm not complaining, but it's not really the kind of thing you want on your doorstep, is it?

I've just sold my bakery. I don't knead the dough anymore.

This bloke accused me of stealing a sign from outside the cafe. I didn't take any notice.

I've a lot on my mind: I'm thinking about buying a car park.

Narrow boats: I wouldn't touch them with a barge pole.

I bumped into Billy the Kid on his way out of McDonalds. I said, fancy a chat? He said, I'd love to, but I've got to shoot...

Someone stole a wheel off my car. I went spare.

I stopped for this hitch-hiker. He said, Crewe...? And seventy-seven ratings from HMS Edinburgh began clambering in the back.

I saw this one-legged, Arctic seabird on its way into the library. I thought, there's a tern hop for the books.

All the instruments in the orchestra had a big fight. All, that is, bar one: the peace cymbal stayed out of it.

I met my new girlfriend online. Her name is Dot...Dot Com.

There was this bloke at court, beating up the ushers. When he'd finished, I said, would you like me to do the honours?

I went for this trainee dentist's job. He said, have you done this kind of work before? I said, yeah, I know the drill.

This sign in the polling station said, place votes here. I queued up for ages behind loads of flat fish, exercising their constitutional rights.

I think my alarm clock has OCD: it won't stop ticking.

It said on my wage slip, tear along the dotted line. So I positioned myself at one end then ran as fast as I could to the far side.

When the weatherman said it was going to be chilly, the last thing I expected was to find the streets coated in red peppers.

I drove round the world in my Honda. I did it in my own Accord.

A sign in the pub said, Gordon's gin, two pounds per glass. I said, the name's Ralph, how much to me?

I watched this film last night, where earth was invaded by a marauding army of walnut whips. It was War of the Whirls.

Strangers in the Night by Frank Sinatra, it's all about a cartoon dog: Scooby dooby doo...

I was watching Miss Universe. The contestant from Brazil came second to Miss Oblok Magellana, constellation Alpha Centauri.

People usually cross over when they see me out with the wife. She's small, thin and sallow-looking, with a big head and black, almond-shaped eyes. In case you wondered, her name is Hayley...Hayley Anne Grey.

I was on the verge of buying a trap door company. But then it all fell through.

That saying, sticks and stones may break my bones but words can never hurt me, I stopped at the garage the other day and a hot pies sign blew down and knocked me clean out.

I arrived at court to find the usher was a dodgem, my solicitor was a big wheel, and the judge was a hook-a-duck stall. I thought, oh well, at least I'll get a fair trial.

Bad tempered monks: they've a real nasty habit.

I've just seen bottles of Tizer, practising with drums and guitars. I thought, whey hey, a pop group.

There's this great Welsh action film on tonight: it's Dai Hard.

I've just been made redundant from my beer sampling job at the brewery. Talk about bitter pill to swallow.

That bloke at work, the one who operates the lathe: he's just been awarded the Turner Prize.

I was working in the launderette when I fell into one of the machines and nearly drowned. The boss didn't half hang me out to dry.

I had an argument with this professor of archaeology. I couldn't believe it: he went absolutely historical.

That documentary the other night, the one about Pickford's: talk about moving.

I'm reading a book about American motorcycle gangs. I'm on the ninety-eighth chapter.

The wife called to say she was bored. When I got home, that's what she was: a thin piece of wood, cut into a square.

I used to be a security man in an underwear factory. I had a watching brief.

Mona Lisa. She was no oil painting.

There was a radio ham in the butchers. It was a pork flavoured walkie-talkie.

I love football. I'm also a forest fan: my favourites are Sherwood and Delamere.

A trio of tiddlywinks are thought to have been responsible for today's foiled bomb plot. Police have now been joined by officers experienced in counter terrorism.

I was messing around on my old CB radio. I said, Rodger, over and out. This voice said, the name's Bob, actually.

The clock in my bedroom goes tick-tick, tick-tick, tick-tick, tick-tick: it's just spent a week in de-tocks.

I went for an interview with a firm specialising in reproduction, medieval decapitation instruments. It was held at the company headquarters: a head, cut into four pieces and impaled on spikes.

There was this group of people, jumping around on one leg, singing songs from HMS Pinafore. I think it was the local hop erratic society.

I had a race with a medieval axe-man. He won by a head.

When I was in the army, I got lost in London. I was missing in Acton.

I was busy raking my front lawn when Mick Jagger suddenly appeared. I said, fancy giving me a hand, Mick? He said, no thanks. I said, why not? He said, a Rolling Stone gathers no moss.

The new CD changer in my car is fantastic. I put a Michelle McManus CD in and it came out The Beatles.

I'm just reading a book by Henry Ford. It's his auto-biography.

There's this troop of mounted soldiers that are afraid to go out in the dark. It's the light cavalry.

It's just been announced that the government is placing a levy on copper and zinc alloy in order to raise revenue. Talk about getting down to brass tax.

He said, you're really gullible, aren't you? I said, am I? What, really?

I said, I got those free tickets. He said, what for? I said, erm, nothing. I got them for nothing...

There was this bloke, tossing a Vauxhall Astra in the air and whacking it with a tennis racket. He was obviously having his car serviced.

I went on an excursion to Berlin and fell out with everyone I met. I must have been having a bad Herr day.

This cowboy drew on me. So I snatched his pen off him and snapped it straight in half.

I stole a pair of cowboy boots. I don't know why. I just did it on the spur of the moment.

Someone asked me if there was a B&Q in Mansfield. I said, I'm not sure, but there's definitely an M and S.

I passed an RAF station, filled with young singles, looking for love. I thought, ooh look, a dater base.

This bloke offered me a lift. I said, no thanks: I live in a bungalow.

I always do the washing up in the bath: I'm out of sink.

My wife always comes home smelling of Roses: she works in a chocolate factory.

Biscuit factory employees: they must be crackers.

I popped down the shops. My stomach exploded.

There was this bloke at the car boot sale, looking really depressed because he hadn't sold a single item off his military replica stall. I said, penny for your forts?

I've fallen in love with my woodworking tools: they're saw adorable.

This bloke rang. He said, is your brother in, the one who's obsessed with hanging himself out with the washing? I said, he is, but I'll have to get him to call you back. He's on the other line at the moment.

I love clip art. I slap people round the face then paint a picture of the shocked expression.

When I was in the army, we all dove for cover when these tortoises began falling on our position. We were being shelled.

The wig factory, it's been robbed again. Police are combing the area.

I had an appointment at the offices of the bloke who invented artificial implants. Interestingly, there's this big bust of him in the foyer.

A huge crater has appeared in the fast lane of the M1. Police are looking into it.

I'm struggling to get the best out of my son. How he managed to swallow a statuette of Man United's famous Irish winger is completely beyond me.

This glass-fronted booth told me the film was cancelled then punched me in the nose. It was a box office.

I saw a bloke with his cheeks on fire. Talk about sideburns.

Packet of Polos for sale. Mint condition.

I fell asleep in a dinghy and woke up half way to Australia. Get my drift?

The Humber Bridge: it's taking its toll.

I went on a plane that had springs instead of wheels and bounced down the runway upon take-off. It was a Boing 747.

The creature off that film, the one where the occupants of an Antarctica research station discover an alien in a block of ice and then fight to stay alive as it consumes them one by one, it's just been on Mastermind. It got thirty questions in a row right then failed on the thirty-first. As the old saying goes: all Things must pass.

I was about to enter this TV competition, when it came on the screen, check with Bill Payer first. I was going to, but in the end I thought, sod it, and just texted in, anyway.

My new girlfriend's surname is Redredrobin. Her first name is Wendy.

I always keep my cool when callers bang on my door while I'm adding the coup de grace to my favourite pie supper, so much so, in fact, I've just been recognised for my restraint by the international community. I've been awarded the no bell peas prize.

The new meat factory: I've got a steak in it.

I was practising at the track when Apollo, Poseidon and Zeus overtook me on the home straight. I thought, crikey, I'm in the lap of the Gods here.

When I was at school, the class created a giant mural of McDonalds. I drew the short straw.

I've just been fired from my human cannonball's job. It's their loss, mind: they'll never find anyone of the same calibre.

That letter I received from the bank, the one telling me my account is empty, I've absolutely no interest.

I finally got an email back from the golf club. Give me five minutes and I'll ping it across to you.

Someone broke in the fancy dress shop and stole the gorilla costume I'd put a deposit on. I went ape when I found out.

I said, doctor, I can't stop repeating my favourite joke. He said, tell me another one.

There was this woman, mopping the office floor and constantly cracking jokes. I thought, whey hey, a dry cleaner.

I was watching the in-flight movie, when this bloke in a red beret suddenly strapped a chute to his back, opened the door and jumped out. Not that anyone paid any attention: it was Para-normal Activity.

Have I ever seen the Abominable Snowman? Not Yeti.

I hit my F1 key: Jenson Button appeared.

Get your mum's sister to marry Robert and, lo and behold, Bob's your uncle.

It was freezing cold on the aeroplane, sitting next to this award-winning American actress. It was Dakota, fanning.

I work in the crisp factory. I'm on a right packet.

General Custer's final words: Look at all them flipping Indians!

I'm vegging out: I'm peeling spuds in the back garden.

Nuisances don't prosper in Hungary. While I was there, all everyone talked about was how they booed-a-pest.

There was this bloke, walking down the street, saying hello, hello, hello, to everyone he met. He must have been on a Hi.

I said, name the fifth Beatle. He said, was it Stag?

While I was in the army, a month of the year tried it on with me: it was forward March.

I went in the travel agents. I said, can I book a flight to Seat, please? She said, never heard of it. I said, what, Seat Ibiza?

There was this spud, swearing its head off at the football match: it was a common-tator.

I've just been to court, accused of robbing the fruiterers'. I got off on a peel.

My new pooh analyser's job isn't going particularly well. Everything I touch turns to disaster. I blame the equipment, but the boss isn't having it: he says a bad worker always blame his stools.

I phoned the Chinese and ordered a house special. Ten minutes later, I was living in a fifteen bedroom mansion with its own swimming pool.

Mummified manic depressives: they're dead miserable.

I phoned Harry Houdini's nephew. This voice said, can you call back later? He's just a bit tied up at the moment.

Alex Ferguson was going to select his kitchen ceiling for Saturday's big game. Unfortunately, it was suspended.

I was in the phone shop. I said, what network do you recommend? He said, orange: loads of pips.

So I said to this bloke, does your dog bite? He said, no. So I went to stroke it and it almost took my fingers off. I said, I thought you said your dog didn't bite? He said, it's not my dog.

I met a bloke made from South African banknotes. How Rand Homme is that?

I used to be a ten pound note. But now I'm a pile of copper. I'm a changed man.

The armed siege at the continental quilt factory: it's getting blanket coverage.

First fly: I live in a cake shop. Second fly: I live in the Tate Gallery. First fly: I can't say I'd care for that. Second fly: Well, you know what they say, don't you? Home is where the art is.

Goole: imagine spending Halloween there.

I went on holiday to Venezuela: I must have been ca-rackers.

Whenever it's raining, I allow Usain Bolt use my car as an indoor arena. You should see him, tearing along my dashboard.

It was raining cats and dogs last night. I should know, I trod in a poodle.

Raining cats and dogs? It was absolutely paw-ring it down.

I said, OK, I'll let you off this time. But don't do anything like that again, do you hear? Then this bloke in a red coat and stupid wig piped up, I'll be the judge of that, thank you.

Let me describe the General picture. It has a gold-painted frame, and depicts some bloke called Wolfe, lying mortally wounded in a red coat, with epaulettes on his shoulder, and medals pinned to his chest.

This sign said, towed caravans prohibited. In the next lay-by, there was a policeman, having a right old row with the driver of a car and caravan he'd stopped. Upon closer inspection, I realised it was Toad from Toad Hall.

I attended the Privet Society AGM. Honestly, I couldn't get a word in hedge ways.

Avoid B-roads at all costs. I didn't and I was stung eighty-seven times.

Metal, plastic and stainless-steel-rimmed: they're on my bucket list.

I attended the Olympic fencing trials but didn't get very far. Perhaps it was because I turned up with my own wire and posts.

When I arrived home from holiday, my IPhone suddenly sprouted wings and began flying round the room. It was still in airplane mode.

I've just been diagnosed with insomnia. Not that I intend losing any sleep over it.

The recession has hit my drapery business so hard, it's looking like curtains.

I fell out with a lift engineer. It was only a minor spat to begin, but quickly escalated.

When I worked in the stationery shop, I used to hate pushy ruler salesmen. Honestly, some of the lengths they'd go to...

I've got a chipped windscreen. I might have it for tea with a battered cod.

The book I was planning, the one about car crashes, don't write it off just yet.

Doctor Hourihane told me to go home and take a tablet. Those Kindle Fires are fantastic, but they don't half take some swallowing.

I was reading the Beano today but didn't understand a word of it: it was the South East Asia Mandarin edition.

Annie reminds me of a bottle of Pernod. It's her surname that's the clincher: it's Seed.

I visited this country, where the entire population spent all day apologising. Talk about a sorry state.

My mate just called to say he's been swallowed by an old bloke down the pub. I know it seems far-fetched, but he did sound like he was talking in Ernest.

I planned to propose to my girlfriend over dinner, but dropped the ring in my rhubarb crumble when she went to the ladies. When I explained what had happened, she said didn't believe me. I told her to please herself: the proof was in the pudding.

These girl squaddies wouldn't stop staring at me. Talk about female atten-shun.

I've just bought a ticking puppy. I think it will make an excellent watchdog.

U-Boat Weekly: I've just sub-scribed.

I thought Tom Daley was a newspaper for alley-cats.

There was this bunch of yobs, beating up a tube of glue. I thought, that's solvent abuse.

I won the lottery then knocked myself out, jumping for joy. Happy daze!

Every time I visit the surgery, I have this enormous sneezing fit. I blame Dr Pepper.

I jumped in this wickerwork basket then carefully untied the rope. That was when the balloon went up.

There was thunder and lightning, going off in my head. I must have been having a brain storm.

I took my car back to the garage, complaining the engine was making a funny noise. They sorted me out in no time: they turned the radio up.

This sign said, workforce in road, slow. I thought, slow, more like snail pace.

I was in the pub when this sheep with wings came in. It was a baa fly.

My brother's crazy about IPhones, IPads and X-Boxes. Not that it bothers me. I just leave him to his own devices.

I witnessed the M5 and the M6, having a right old tear up. I thought, ooh look, cross roads.

All the cars heading over the bridge were driven by blue bottles. It was a fly over.

I adore breakfast TV. I usually have a piece of toasted screen, with scrambled egg and a dab of brown sauce.

OK, so Joe blogs...so what about it?

I was rushed to hospital after accidentally swallowing a mouthful of maggots while fishing. How's it looking, doc? I said, through baited breath...

After a spate of wading bird thefts, a thirty-three year old male has today been charged with storking.

My wife's so materialistic. She arrived home yesterday with sixteen rolls of cloth.

I saw this Golden Retriever, singing Camptown Races en route to summer camp. I thought, ooh look, a guide dog.

Oil salesmen: boy, they're slick.

I had a blazing row with the new office junior. I told him to get his fax straight.

The railway station was closed and His Royal Highness wasn't amused. I thought, ooh look, King's cross.

Jacuzzi and Uzi 9mm: separated at birth?

I said, what are you babbling on about? He said, I can hear a brook.

People locked in dark rooms: I really feel for them.

I love my pet Brazil nuts. When I go on holiday, I put them in the boarding kernels.

My new girlfriend showed up in fish-net tights. I thought, oh my cod!

Teacher: define context. Pupil: is it a bad joke from your mate in prison?

I was summoned to school after my son had his pea-shooter confiscated. The teacher described it as a weapon of maths disruption.

This American soul group phoned to say they were working their way back to me, babe, with a burning love inside. Surprise, surprise, they never turned up. But at least now I know why they're called the Detroit Spinners.

I had a brilliant business, manufacturing toilet seats. Then the bottom fell out of it.

Elephant hide: it's a grey area.

There was this bloke at work today, who couldn't stop reciting Shakespeare. He was having a Bard day at the office.

I spent June, July and August eating kebabs, whilst singing I Feel Love and Hot Stuff. It was my Donna Summer.

Toothless Rottweiler's: their bark is worse than its bite.

I booked some swimming lessons but wish I hadn't bothered. It was a load of blokes in trunks, practising underwater algebra.

An enemy aircraft was shot down today by a flying egg. Due to government cutbacks, calls to scramble are now being handled by RAF cooks.

I saw this frog, getting ready to jump off London Bridge. I thought, he's going to Kermit suicide.

That young couple who threw themselves off the cliff, I always said their marriage was on the rocks.

I didn't get that job at the snakes & ladders factory: now I'm back to square one.

The pig farm's practically mine. I'm just waiting for the oink to dry.

My new job in elastic band design, it's alright, but I can't say it stretches me.

I started this new telesales job and all my colleagues were ex-miners. It was a coal centre.

There was this bloke on the market, selling Venison. I said, is it dear?

I was on holiday in Benidorm. This waiter said, full English? I said, I might be, Spanish, if you ever fetch my breakfast.

The sliced Hovis at the pool yesterday, it was the loafguard.

I can't believe a sewing machine actually won X Factor. Credit where credit's due, though: it was a brilliant Singer.

The wife surprised me with a new puppy. I just stood there in aww.

I walk the dog in a coat made from King Edwards, Jersey Royals and Maris Pipers. It's my jacket potato.

Inflation is getting ridiculous. I bought a bag of nuts and it cost me an almond a leg.

My new jigsaw factory: the pieces are starting to come together at last.

I took a bath in baked beans for charity. But it didn't half leave me feeling sore. Next time, I think I might try taking them out of the tins.

This sign said, weak bridge ahead. When I got there, there was this puny bridge, doing bench presses, mentored by a personal trainer.

I was on the eighteenth green when this car went flying over my head and demolished the clubhouse. I thought, aye-aye, someone's playing Volkswagen Golf again.

Did you hear about the paper cowboy? He had a paper hat, paper waistcoat, paper shirt, paper trousers, and paper boots. He even had a paper gun and holster. They hung him for rustling.

I adore my pet battery. You may have heard me in the park, training it. Stay, Positive.

Puppet show free to good home. No strings attached.

I heard this shrieking noise coming from my six-pack. Straight after, I was running to the toilet. Talk about screaming ab-dabs.

When I announced I'd enrolled my son at prop school, this bloke said, don't you mean prep school? I said, actually, no, he's in the same class as a Spitfire and a Wellington bomber.

I boarded this flight and all the passengers and crew were wearing beards and moustaches. It was a hairy plane.

The boss told me to pop the bubble wrap delivery in the corner. Fifteen blooming hours it took.

I've just bought a house on a street with no name. No sweat, though: I can always address it later.

My new milk round in Liverpool: it doesn't half take some Bootle.

I was watching Newsnight when the PM's chair caught fire. Talk about being in the hot seat.

People who live in Towcester: I bet I know what they have for breakfast.

I've just been banned from the pool for dive-bombing. I knew I should have left the Stuka at home.

This widescreen plasma was chasing me down the street and gaining fast. It was then I realised: it was catch-up TV.

I booked in with this driving school. Imagine the shock I got when St Winifred's Junior & Infants science block turned up in a Ford Focus.

My next door neighbour, Michael, the one who works at the earthquake research institute, he hasn't half clapped weight on. Talk about size-Mick-shift.

I saw this bloke from the council, measuring the perimeter of a field full of ponies. It must have been something to do with the latest batch of horse territory measures.

I put my Crippen costume on last night. I was dressed to kill.

There was this bloke on the beach and he had big, pointed ears with a thick mane of hair going down the back of his neck. As I watched him fire-up the barbie, then whip the top off a can of Fosters, I thought, whey hey, an horse-tralian.

My friend reckons he's the new MD at the wool factory. What a yarn.

I was going to set up a company importing dog harnesses, but the lead times were ridiculous.

None of the cash machines are working in York. The River Ouse has broken its banks.

I've written a book about boggy marshlands. Available from all good bookstores, it's a superb reed.

It's that time of year again, the time when I have to go before the boss to praise some geezer called Al.

My book about the meaning of life: I wrote it on the 7.22 from Sheffield to London, St Pancras. Talk about a train of thought.

I bought some pork flavoured condiment. It was Peppa Pig.

Every time I cut the grass, the size of my garden doubles. I blame the lawn more.

I used to work for KP. The pay was peanuts.

Did you hear about the investigative journalist who couldn't stop breaking wind? He was a right pooper-scooper.

I have a job with five-thousand people under me. I cut grass in the cemetery.

There's a hangman's job going at the prison. Leave it with me, and I'll make sure you're kept in the loop.

I got out of prison and went straight...to bed.

There was this bloke in the pub last night and his trouser legs were on fire. He was wearing flares.

I stumbled across this barbed wire prison, where all the inmates were strolling around with furrowed brows. It was a concentration camp.

That twenty foot wall: someone says there's a nudist camp on the other side. But I can't see it myself.

I put the kettle on. But I can't say it suited me.

I popped in this factory shop. I bought a big, red-brick building with two tall chimneys.

This sign said, all unauthorised vehicles will be clamped. When I got back from shopping, my Vauxhall Corsa was covered in slimy molluscs.

People refer to me as the big cheese: I'm manager at the dairy.

I phoned this crane hire company. They sent me a grey bird with long legs and curved tail feathers.

My hospital scan was undertaken by the scariest, six-foot bear I've ever seen. X-ray-Ted didn't come into it.

I couldn't believe it when United announced their new centre half was a three-bedroomed, semi-detached. But it did bring a whole new meaning to the term house clearance.

When I was in the navy, we discovered a Pacific atoll filled with rancid puddings and old vinyl. It was dessert island discs.

I bumped into this squaddie, walking down the street with a Golden Labrador strung round his neck. It must have been his dog tag.

The wife bought me a camel for Christmas when she knew all along I wanted a giraffe. I didn't half get the hump with her.

I was in this restaurant when a Red Indian walked in. The waiter said, do you have a reservation? He said, actually, no, I live in the council flats on King's Road.

My new pine furniture: I'm sick of hearing it bleat on about its days in the forest.

I was working at the checkout when this monk had problems with his credit card. As I recall, it was something to do with the ex-priory date.

The weather forecasters reckon it won't rain for six months: but I drought it.

I was in this meeting when the manager suddenly poured mushy peas over the pie chart and had it for dinner.

People tell me I'm gifted. Perhaps it's something to do with the fact I'm permanently swathed in sheets of Christmas wrapping paper.

I went to work with one glove on and one glove off. It was the weatherman's fault. He said it might be cold. Or, on the other hand, it could be sunny.

My two buoys are all grown up now. They're currently anchored in the North Sea, channelling maritime traffic.

I'm embarked upon a joint venture: I'm starting up a hip replacement company.

Things are picking up. I've just been offered that job at the Hoover factory.

I've just seen Mr Kipling out with his wife. What a tart.

Hypodermic needles: they get under my skin.

I've just had a brush with the law. I whacked this PC round the head with a broom.

A friend offered me a hundred pounds to wallpaper his flat for him. I told him I'd rather hang myself first.

I'm a compulsive lier...I spend all day flat out up in bed.

Skin surgeons: they're real grafters.

Angus took time off work with a tickly throat. In actual fact, it was a wee cough.

I joined the local operatic society, but fell through a trap door during my debut performance. It happened again on the second night, and then again on the third. Not that I let it affect my confidence. It was just a stage I was going through.

When I was at university, I had this twelve month period when all I did was stare at people. It was my gape year.

The stress at the egg farm: I'm not sure I can coop anymore.

I was having a game of pontoon when the ten of diamonds started growling at me. Talk about a wild card.

There's this institution near me, where football pitches go when they aren't feeling very well. It's the field hospital.

I'm trying to learn the guitar. But it's really slow on the uptake.

OK, so my alter ego keeps calling me names. I refuse to beat myself up about it.

A bloke in just his underwear shouted me over and explained he was Sherlock Holmes in disguise. I thought, many a sleuth spoken in vest.

I bought these new running shoes that reeked of 5 star unleaded. I thought, whey hey, petrol pumps.

Red Indians: they say it How it is.

I was checking out new cars. I said, what's this dial for? He said, it keeps a tally of how many vicars you drive past during a set period. I said, that will be the Rev counter, then?

A sign in the pub said, after shocks, a pound each. So I paid the barman and the ground started shaking under my feet.

The sign in the window said, trousers, a fiver. I went straight in and ordered sixteen pairs. How the heck was I supposed to know it was the dry cleaners?

I love irritating people. And, if at first I don't succeed, I always have a get somebody's back up plan.

There was this film on last night about two opposing armies, exchanging pleasantries. It was set in the civil war.

I was working as a security guard when I spotted this bloke, stuffing a cuckoo clock up his jumper. I got to him in the nick of time.

All I could afford for the wife's birthday was an old, second-hand clock. She said, is this a wind-up?

I've just seen this small dog, giving its owner a right telling off. It was a Jack Russell, cross.

A general strike's been called. The army is in chaos.

I heard this cat, reciting poetry. I thought, that's purr-verse.

They wouldn't let my dad in the pub because he had a plate of Tom Yam Goong balanced on his head. I said, you can't do that: it's a Pa Thaied...

I followed a signpost for Potters Bar. When I got there, it was loads of snooker players, playing cards and drinking beer.

My dentist drilled so hard he set my mouth on fire. Talk about burning his bridges.

I'm off on a right do tonight, two quid in, drink as much as you like. If you fancy coming along, the swimming baths opens at six.

This starving cannibal said he was going to eat my ticker. I thought, he's a man after my own heart.

I used to be a racehorse trainer. I was on the left hoof, back leg, white, with a plastic Nike symbol across the heel.

An Australian lorry driver is to be prosecuted after he spilled his load of brooms on the M1. The brush trucker trial is due to start next week.

I said, doctor, I went blind on the train, but my sight returned the instant we entered the dark bits. He said, you've got tunnel vision.

That clock repairer's job, I turned it down in the end. I didn't think the time was right.

I took a straw exam: I got an hay.

We've had a new tank installed in the loft. It's a British Army surplus Challenger 2.

I said, I'd like to see a doctor, please. She said, which doctor? I said, witch doctor? Where's Doctor Hourihane, then?

My ex-wife used to be a diesel fitter. She'd trail round clothes shops with my daughter and credit card, saying diesel fitter, diesel fitter...

I was taking a history degree but packed it in after the first week. I couldn't see any future in it.

So, we're all agreed: there's sixty seconds per minute, sixty minutes per hour, and twenty-four hours in the period during which the earth makes one rotation on its axis...now then, shall we call it a day?

I'm off to Rome this weekend...roam round the back garden.

This inebriated electrician turned up at my house, swigging on a bottle of whisky. I think he was trying to pliers with drink.

I've just bought a new poacher's coat. It cost me a pocket.

A spud just told me how nice I looked: sweet potato.

I went in WH Smith, and there were these two bestsellers, having a punch-up. It must have been a title fight.

The forecast said, increasing cloud towards dawn. When I got home, there was Dawn, backing off across the kitchen to escape the attentions an approaching fair weather cumulus.

Ayr United have placed Dan Druff on the transfer list. Word is Barnet are after him.

This bloke rang to say my car radio had been repaired. It was like music to my ears.

I went in the garden and there was this growling flower in a blonde wig and long dress. I think it was Lily Savage.

The vicar organised a charity cricket match in the bell tower. Talk about bats in the belfry.

I can feel myself being slowly drawn towards Mecca: it's the new bingo house round the corner.

The wife wasn't happy when she found tele upside down. I can't understand her: she was the one who told me to turn it over.

I've just heard a car barking. It was a Rover.

We didn't know what to call our new puppy until it attacked this burglar. When he screamed, call the dog Hoff, we thought, what a great idea, and named him after that bloke on Baywatch.

I used to be king of the castle, but now I'm just a water-filled ditch. I've been de-moated.

When I leave school, I want to be a lollipop man: word is they don't start until they are sixty-five.

I couldn't believe it when it started raining chancellors. Talk about economic climate.

There was this woman with a map of a Belgian city painted on her cheeks. I suppose it was her Bruges.

I poured Domestos all over a fresh fruit display in the supermarket. I was charged with bleach of the peach.

A sign on this ice-cream van said, slow watch for children. I thought, no way: they'll be late for school.

I spent my day off in the pool, drifting on my back. It was a floating holiday.

Apparently there are thousands of jobs going begging in London. Trouble is, who wants to go begging in London?

I went to the Natural History Museum and asked the curator what he could tell me about T Rex. He said, the lead singer was Marc Bolan and they had a number one hit with Hot Love.

Whenever my mother's sister wins the pub quiz, she celebrates by dressing up as a digital alarm. She's my aunty clock wise.

I went to a cake eating contest yesterday. Talk about Battenburg down the hatches.

Every time the sun comes out, my new Ford bursts into song. I've never owned a ray-sing car before.

I upset this shoe. Talk about putting my foot in it.

My Samurai sword business is in trouble. I've no cutting edge.

A friend of mine reckons he got into an argument with Mr Burgin at the chippie, who belted him round the face with a piece of wet fish. If you ask me, it's a right load of codswallop.

I sent my six-year old for a box of teabags, but the woman at the shop wouldn't serve him. Apparently the PG in Tips means parental guidance.

I was caned so many times at school, I started to think my name was Ben Dover.

This bottle of kitchen cleaner just exposed itself to me: it was the Flash cream.

My chimney sweep pulled a rabbit out of his hat then turned my cat into a frog. I'm sick of him and his dirty tricks.

I've called in sick so many times, next time I'm going to have to tell them I've snuffed it.

A friend of mine reckons he owns fifty venomous snakes. Personally, I think it's a right load of cobras.

There was this sign saying, staggered junction. I thought, not as staggered as I am with the amount of time the roadworks are taking.

I put the boxing on and there was this fighter, sparring in a trilby. It was Ricky Hat On.

My best friend at school was a paper boy. He blew away.

I've just seen Winnie the Pooh walk into a wall. Talk about a bear with a sore head.

I ran a bath last night. I chased it out of B&Q and off down the street.

Teacher: what did I do with my cane? Pupil: Beats me!

I was visiting Kew Gardens when Mick Jagger went flying through the air and demolished a display of winter pansies. People in glass houses shouldn't throw Stones.

I'm an aerial photographer. I take pictures of boxes of my favourite washing powder.

The boss ordered me to shovel twenty tons of coal from one cellar to another. I thought, give me strength.

When I was naughty, my dad always gave me a belt. I have nine hundred and sixty-three of the infernal things, cluttering up the wardrobe.

I went to Stratford upon Avon and was chased down the street by some cannibal called William, shaking a spear.

Question 22 in the pub quiz: which film featured the songs Happy Talk and Wonderful Guy? I said, can you be a bit more spacific...?

I was heading up the motorway when I spotted this giant protractor on a hill. It was the Angle of the North.

Twenty plus thirty and forty plus ten: it's fifty-fifty.

I went in the kitchen and there was this big, black cloud, putting the kettle on. It was a storm brewing.

This bloke said, you'll never get your joke book published. I said, funnier things have happened...

I moved in with that old woman, the one who lives in a shoe. When I complained to her about the lack of privacy, she told me to zip it: we were all in the same boot.

A man burst into a supermarket last night and brutally assaulted boxes of Cornflakes, Weetabix, Coco Pops and Shreddies. Police believe a cereal killer may be on the loose.

I bought a job lot of hangman's nooses and sold the lot on Ebay. It was money for old rope.

The heist at the art gallery: I'm definitely in the frame.

I saw dozens of small, rounded stones, having a race. I thought, whey hey, a pebble dash.

These government cuts are really starting to take effect: new canals are appearing all over the place.

I got straight on the phone to the wife when I arrived home to find the kitchen filled with glass-filled, wooden frames. I said, have you been window shopping again?

Bespectacled business people in pinstripe suits: they're definitely behind The Times.

I've just had my staircase decorated: it won a George Cross for storming a machine-gun nest, single-handed.

There was this coconut-filled chocolate bar, being chased down the street by a gun-toting cowboy, clutching a rolled-up wanted poster. I thought, whey hey, a Bounty hunter.

I'm writing a book about wind turbines. My publisher loves the first draught.

We always go on holiday by bus or car: never the twain.

I was working behind the bar when this party came in from the Band-Aid factory. You should have seen them by the end of the night: they were well plastered.

There was this bottle of Lemonade in the pub, knocking back double whiskies. It must have been an alco-pop.

I went to the swimming baths, and there was this Vauxhall Vectra, doing the back-stroke. This sales rep said it was his pool car.

Me and my best mate, the reformed pyromaniac: we get on like a house on fire.

I overlaid this morning. I woke up and the bedroom was filled with eggs.

My sister is marrying a Pampers salesman. Let's hope they live nappily ever after.

I came down with the latest strain of influenza virus A. Next day, the wife had it as well. I said, don't worry, we'll get flu this.

The cashier couldn't scan my Shaun the Sheep rucksack. No baa code.

I was going to retire, but changed my mind after a trip to Anfield. All through the game, the crowd were singing, work on, work on, with hope in your heart...

There were these pop stars in the fancy dress shop, dressing up as characters from the Wizard of Oz. Madonna was Dorothy, Robbie Williams was Tin Man and Gary Barlow the Scarecrow. I thought, whey hey, the lion's Cher.

I applied for that job at the laundry. I thought I'd strike while the iron was hot.

Hamburger please, I said...with relish.

If Walls had ears, there wouldn't be any sausages, because they would all disappear the instant anyone mentioned frying pan.

My girlfriend owns her own chemist shop, ploughs fields in her spare time and giggles hysterically when I poke her in the ribs. She's farmer-Sue-tickle.

I've been pepper-sprayed sixteen times since I left the army. I'm a seasoned veteran.

Bad tempered electricians: short fuse doesn't come into it.

That new natural history museum was a bit of a disappointment. All they had was the skeleton of a giant Grizzly. I thought, crikey, we're down to the bear bones here.

Some men from outer space stole my six-pack. It was a clear case of alien ab-duction.

My next door neighbour was banging my door down at three in the morning. It was a good job I was still up, practising my bagpipes.

I was visiting the zoo when someone said this tall animal with a long neck was about to give birth. I said, you're having a giraffe.

Absent minded authors: they've lost the plot.

I helped my illiterate mate fill a form in yesterday. We went in the park and beat this bench up.

An armed siege is taking place at an ice-cream parlour in Torquay. Police have coned off the area.

I'm disqualified from driving: my balls keep flying through the clubhouse window.

He's a right big head. Humpty Dumpty.

I could tell you this joke about sweaty feet. But I'd better not: it's too corny.

My pal's got his hands on a box of knock-off laptops. I've offered him fifty quid for one, but he hasn't come back to me yet. I suppose it's up to him: he holds all the Acers.

I was going to buy a Labrador but changed my mind. Everyone I know who's ever owned one has gone blind.

I drove my car into quicksand. Don't ask me how I feel: it hasn't sunk in yet.

OK, so they're busy renovating the hotel. But I don't think it's right the porters should have to use an outside loo.

I'm a Vietnam Vet. I look after sick animals in Hanoi.

It said in the paper there are ten thousand jobs in Jeopardy: but can I heckers like find it anywhere on the map.

Did you know that Elizabeth Taylor's husband once rowed a boat down a river in Staffordshire? They even named a town after the event: it's Burton upon Trent.

I went in Tesco's and couldn't believe how much whisky was reserved for some bloke called Jack Daniels.

A coup has taken place...in the pigeon loft.

I bought this fantastic Mexican carpet. But can't say I thought much to the underlay, underlay!

One man bands: it's time they got their act together.

B&Q's gardening department: it's cutting hedge.

I filled up at this Gulf garage. The cashier wasn't talking to the manager, and all the customers were staring daggers at one another.

Mr Whippy turned up in his new van, I thought, he's changed his tune.

That table I booked for Valentine's Day, what a disaster...the wife didn't pot a single ball.

I had a pizza made from bits of skyscraper last night: it was Chicago town.

My brother Will joined the army but left because the officers kept telling everyone to fire at him.

That rumour going round, the one about me being addicted to dilute orange: just for the record, I'd like to quosh it.

I had an ice-cream sundae. I had one on Monday as well, and another Tuesday.

Calendars: their days are numbered.

This sign outside the pub said, free pool all day. I felt such an idiot when I turned up in my cossie and everyone was playing eight-ball.

I have my own ceramics business and write poetry in my spare time. No one can accuse me of not being verse-a-tile.

As we filed off the bus in Amsterdam, this tour guide kept saying, welcome to Holland, welcome to Holland. She was talking double Dutch.

This bloke ran in my house. He said, do, any Dalmatians live here? It was a spot check.

I lost my job at the tennis ball factory. Not worries, though: I'll soon bounce back.

Gutted I'd fallen out with my mass murderer mate, the one who always chops his victims into a thousand pieces, I phoned him up and said, look, can't we just bury the hatchet?

I gave up my nude modelling career. I was barely making a living.

There was this motor vehicle down the disco, chatting all the girls up. I thought, whey hey, a pick-up truck.

I work for a blue chip company. We make frozen fries for the UK's Smurf community.

Budgie for sale. Going cheap.

There was this bloke with people behind his eyes, operating computers, printing invoices and having meetings. When I asked him about it, he explained it was his head office.

Everyone must think my wife is an expert in ancient Chinese porcelain. I've lost count of the number of times people have said, I see you're still married to that Ming-er.

I've just won the Ryder Cup. I caught four hundred and sixteen buses in a day.

Did you see the big film last night, the one about murderous, cannibalistic molluscs? It was Silence of the Clams.

I sold my PC and got a Mac. At least it keeps me dry in the rain.

Angus was in danger of being extradited but got off on appeal. Apparently it would have infringed his Hoot Mon rights.

I'm addicted to wheel trims. I've just been booked in to re-hub.

The memorial factory where I worked has finally closed its doors. For the first time in my life, I'm urn employed.

I made a fortune from selling savoury potato cakes. Then I just frittered it all away.

My new back door: there's got to be a catch to it.

Driving through Derbyshire, I couldn't help noticing that everyone was wearing hats with visors. But then I was in the Peak District.

I collate information on speech impediments. I'm a stutter-stician.

There was this tin of meat being picked on by another tin of meat. It was bully beef.

I've just seen Ringo Starr in the park, practising amongst the hydrangeas. Talk about beating around the bush.

St George. Don't believe a word he slays.

I'm a bit below par today. I'm at the foot of the mountain and my dad is at the top.

Frozen apples: they're hard core.

My pooch talks in her sleep. And she's always economical with the truth. No sweat, though: let sleeping dogs lie is what I say.

I came across a sign saying, Men at Work. When I turned the corner, it was eighties' Australian rock band, singing a song called Land Down Under.

The doctor sent me to hospital for an op'. When I got there, they made me stand on one leg then skip down a corridor.

I got wasted last night. This bloated cannibal left me on the side of his plate.

This bloke called. He said, I hear you've a counterfeiting machine that needs repairing, would you mind if I left you my number? I said, hang on a sec' and I'll make a note of it.

Twenty minutes later, it was back working again. I said to him, Sterling work!

My wife ran screaming from the bathroom, convinced someone called Matthew had collapsed on the floor. I told her not to be silly. It was just the bath Matt.

I once knew a deaf fisherman: he was hard of herring.

This collier attacked me. I escaped with miner injuries.

I stepped off this flight to discover my hair had suddenly developed a perm. It's the last time you'll catch me flying with British airwaves.

Bram Stoker: you can't count on him.

I was once a movie star. That bit in Titanic, when the lifeboats are out, if you look in the top left hand corner, you can just see me, twinkling.

Did you hear about the eighty-eight year old German footballer who scored three times? It was a geriatric Jerry hat-trick.

I saw a sign saying, road ahead blocked. When I got there, that's what it was, a road, shaped like a head, with a runny nose.

My wheat farm doesn't half give me a headache. But at least it's my grain.

I said, doctor, I've got a cricket ball stuck up my rear end. He said, how's that? I said, don't you start!

Madonna has agreed to star in a new film about the Vietnam War. It's going to be called, A Puck Her Lips Now.

I went on this crash course. The instructor said, accelerate to sixty miles per hour and aim for that wall.

Gary Barlow and Robbie Williams have been accused of stealing a packet of chocolate digestives. I thought, well, that just about Take That takes the biscuit.

I got up this morning and the wife was foaming at the mouth. I thought, oh no, she's eaten her blooming pillow again

My mate said there was no one on the Jonathan Ross Show last night. I thought, that must have been interesting, listening Jonathan Ross, rabitting away to himself.

I was really keen on this new house until the estate agent informed me there was no chain. I said, what about when I want to flush the toilet?

That book I wrote about underground rooms, brimming with coal: it's a best cellar.

I bought the wife a watch for her birthday and asked for it wrapping. Big mistake: when I got it home, could I heckers like stop it chanting rhyming lyrics.

Did you know Count Dracula has a cousin that makes people so scared they begin to sneeze? He's the Pollen Count.

I'm reading this brilliant book about sponges. Absorbing doesn't come into it.

Manual labour: is it the President of Argentina?

This bloke called me chicken. I told him to stop using fowl language.

I said, doctor, I've started dreaming in colour. He said, it's just a pigment of your imagination.

A couple of budgies started work on the factory production line. I thought, whey hey, cheap labour.

I asked my Texan girlfriend which German car she preferred. She said, Audi partner.

That new complaints box they've installed at work: it told me it didn't like my tie.

I've just had a piggy back. My prize boar was stolen then anonymously returned two hours later.

I saw a bull, reading a bible. I thought, holy cow.

That bloke who looks after that goat herd in the field behind my house isn't half temperamental. He needs treating with kid's gloves.

I used to be a waiter in a restaurant across the road from a bookies shop. The wages weren't great. But the tips were fantastic.

If you receive an email saying you can catch Swine Flu from tins of ham, just delete it. It's Spam.

This bloke said, have you heard the one about...and then he puked all over himself. I thought, whey hey, a sick joke.

I live in a high rise apartment, constructed from piles of deflated inner tubes. It's a block of flats.

No one complained when I had a skip outside my house. The trouble started when I painted a hopscotch grid on the pavement.

Howard Webb went into a hotel. He said, I'd like to book a room, please.

I came across a sign saying, bends for ten miles. I counted a hundred and thirteen divers, suffering decompression symptoms.

There was this bloke, busy nailing arms and legs to a torso. I thought, whey hey, a body builder.

I went to see Steps last night. There's no denying it: B&Q have a fantastic selection.

This bloke accused me of stealing his fish and chips. I took it with a pinch of salt.

I was in this butcher's shop in Derbyshire. This woman said, is that turkey, duck? Her husband said, no, duck, that's chicken, duck. They left with a joint of beef and a stick of black pudding.

Teacher: What did you do on bonfire night? Boy: Shoved bangers up pigeon's backsides, miss. Teacher: Backsides?

Do you mean rectum? Boy: Rectum? It blew their blooming heads off!

I struck a happy medium last night. I clouted a grinning fortune teller.

As the mayoral parade came to end, the town crier put in an appearance. It was all over bar the shouting.

I paid this chef a tenner to top my conifers. Waste of money. All he did was sprinkle them with grated cheese.

So I said to my eighteen inch friend, the one with the lizard's tail and ears like a donkey, what exactly did you say to Harry Potter?

They're making a film about a golfing magician. It will be called Harry Putter.

I bought my daughter a hula hoop but all it did was growl at her. Talk about vicious circle.

There was this sign saying, heavy plant crossing. Next thing, a twenty stone yucca walked in front of my car.

I drew the curtains. But the rest of the furniture in the room is real.

Boiled eggs: you can't beat them.

I turned down that job at the chippie: I had other fish to fry.

So I said, no, it was Ringo Starr, do you hear me? Ringo Starr, I say! Honestly, some people: you have to drum it into them!

I've invented a new kind of brush. It's sweeping the nation.

Jimmy White and Steve Davis. They've gone to pot.

The woman in the woodshop, the one who operates the lathe, whilst singing Simply the Best all day: she's Turner Tina.

I saw the Royal Oak, enjoying lunch with the St George's Arms. They were in a pub restaurant.

Hum, drone, murmur, whine and whirr: they're real buzz words.

I've just seen a bloke, wearing a jacket made from Arctic sea birds. I thought, what a tern coat.

They're selling cows cheap on the market. I was going to buy one till I realised they were all non-branded.

I have an extremely stable home life. I live in this shelter, previously occupied by racehorses.

Rooney placed the ball in the quadrant then stepped back to make way for the bread van. It was delivering to the corner shop.

I created merry hell when my B&Q delivery arrived on a set of false teeth. I said to the driver, I never asked for it delivering by pallet.

Circuses: they're not fair.

Every time I visit my caravan, my hair stands on end: it's a static.

I have wooden legs and a rickety back. I also own my own company. In actual fact, I'm the chair man.

What did former Prime Ministers Harold Wilson and Ted Heath have in common? They both smoked a pipe except for Ted Heath.

I've just been dragged one thousand seven hundred and sixty yards behind a moving car. I certainly arrived with a mile on my face.

The receptionist at the orange juice factory: I've got a crush on her.

I got that job at the glue factory. All I need to do now is make sure I apply myself.

There's this city in France, where the inhabitants are either falling asleep with nothing to do, or rolling around, laughing like crazy. It's bored-ho.

I gave this bloke fifty pence for charity. Next thing, he was pinning a new-born dog to my chest. I said, I didn't know it was puppy day.

King Harold's final words: when will eye be famous?

I couldn't get into Andy Capp's autobiography. There was no Flo to it.

That woman down at the dress-makers shop, the one who fancies herself as a comedian: she definitely needs some new material.

I said to this bloke, put your money where your mouth is. And so he ate his wallet.

I went to the chemists, and that girl was in again, the one who used to work at McDonalds. I said, can I have a box of laxatives, please? She said, to go? I said, what do you think?

Question one in last night's pop quiz: who invented Tizer?

I was invited to a funeral at 6am but never turned up. I'm not really a mourning person.

When I split from the wife, she made a bonfire from all the clothes I'd bought her. A few weeks later, she begged me to take her back. I told her no chance. As far as I was concerned, she'd burned her britches.

I'm always screwing up at work. I make my living fitting electric ceiling fans.

This bloke at the pub was adamant he'd had an original Rembrandt passed down to him. What he didn't tell us was that it was passed down to him from a bedroom window.

I thought I was feeling a bit off colour, but realised I didn't know the meaning of the phrase until I'd forced down that blooming medicine ball.

Schooldays: I never did come to terms with them.

I was charged with possession of a live hand grenade. It was thrown out of court.

Alley cats: they're definitely feline the pinch.

I phoned the wife and asked if she fancied going out later. She said she was too tired. When I got home, I realised what she meant: she'd only turned into a flipping racing bike.

A sign in the pub said, four shots, five pounds. So I gave the barman a fiver then blew his head off.

I went to Paris and jumped into this big river. I must have been in Seine.

What's blue and white and sits in a kitchen? A fridge with a Wrangler on.

I lent that presenter bloke off I'm a Celebrity Get Me out of Here a pair of my trousers. When I saw him out later, I thought, whey hey, Ant's in my pants.

Frankenstein, Werewolf and the Mummy went to the pub for a steak. Dracula never turned up.

I stayed at this strange hotel recently. Every morning, the catering staff could be found playing tennis with bacon, eggs, sausage and beans. Apparently they were serving breakfast.

Things aren't going well at the egg farm. We're struggling to make hens meet.

I started work at the sandwich shop. I said, OK, what's my roll...?

This advert said, cash on delivery, so I got on the phone and ordered two tons of fresh manure. When the driver had tipped, he gave me seventy five quid.

I was born Down Under: I quickly changed my name to John Smith.

People thought I was stupid, packing in my detective's job. It was like I said at the time: what else did I have to prove?

I was walking my dog on Salisbury Plain when this tank started swearing at me. I think it had turrets.

Horticulture: I really dig it.

I saw this bloke fall out of the church tower today. I thought it was the vicar at first. Then I realised: it was just a dead ringer.

The sergeant asked what I'd done with all the fake bullets. I said I couldn't remember: my mind was a blank.

I went in HMV. I said, you don't have The Carpenters in, do you? He said, no, but there's a bloke out back, unblocking the toilet.

That bloke off Baywatch, the Britain's Got Talent judge, the wife's just paid fifty quid for a torn-in-half, autographed picture of him. I thought, what a rip Hoff.

I was on the beach when this car pulled up, and all these gangsters jumped out, and began Tommy-gunning the sea. It was a drive buoy shooting.

OK, so my dog won't stop barking: stop hounding me about it.

I resigned from the colander factory. I couldn't take the strain anymore.

Farmer Giles was viciously assaulted in the chicken coop this morning. Police have refused to rule out fowl play.

Whenever I'm feeling blue, I snack on bottles of fabric conditioner. I'm a Comfort eater.

I said, did you know I've just become an ankle? He said, don't you mean uncle? I said, no, ankle. I'm the joint between this bloke's leg and his foot.

We were on the verge of moving to Iceland. Then the wife got cold feet.

I was in the bathroom showroom when this bloke hurled a toilet through the window. What a crackpot.

Dodgy engines: don't get me started.

I switched my laptop on then hit the shift key. Next thing, I was back at work, just clocking on.

Muhammad Ali figurine for sale. Not boxed.

I've started work as a deckchair attendant. I'm as happy as a sandboy.

That documentary last night, the one about sickness and diarrhoea: it brought it all back.

I was on a tour of the KP factory when Sacha Baron Cohen made a guest appearance, handing out samples. I said, no thanks, I've got a nut Ali G.

Wealthy people always get their own way. It's the law of have riches.

I saw a sign saying, Leek 19 miles. I thought, yeah, right, and pulled up sharpish, nipping behind a tree.

My first night as a security guard at the Hi-vis jacket factory, and half the stock was stolen. Thankfully, the boss said it was no reflection on me.

I asked a female tyre fitter out on a date. She turned me down...flat.

This bloke asked me my birthday. I said, seventeenth of November. He said, what year? I said, every year.

At our last sales meeting, the manager machine-gunned the wall. Talk about bullet points.

I've bought an all terrain vehicle. It looks like the Flying Scotsman and has ten carriages.

My siblings and I have set up a company manufacturing staircases. Well, not siblings exactly: more like step brothers.

I ordered too much orange pop for the shop and had to get a mate in to help me unload. As the saying goes, it takes two to Tango.

That duck I stole: I reckon I'm going down for it.

I went to buy a new watch. The assistant said, Seiko? I said, of quartz.

Workers at the Met Office: they've called a lightning strike.

I saw a flying saucer land in a field, and this bug-eyed monster got out and started eating grass. It must have been one of those alien graze.

Luke Skywalker: what planet is he on?

I went in this second hand shop. I said, what did you do with all the watches, then?

That Jim bloke, the one who owns all the fitness clubs, he must be worth an absolute fortune. If you're not sure who I mean, I think you'll find his surname is Nasium.

I arranged for this woman to come round to shorten my trousers. She never turned up.

For sale: eighteenth century, sixteen bedroom mansion in fifty acres of land, adjacent to cemetery overspill. Location: Causton Town, Midsomer. Offers around: fifty pence for quick sale.

I went to Stratford upon Avon and there was this bloke, carrying a sceptre and wearing a crown, who wouldn't stop staring at me. Someone said it was King Leer.

I bought a new car and they gave me a pamphlet on chopped wood. It was the log book.

Why did the movie crazy chicken cross the road? To see Gregory Peck.

I was enjoying a slap up meal when my mate rang, asking if I fancied a round of golf. I said, I'd love to, but I've a lot on my plate at the moment.

There was this sign saying, keep off the grass. I thought, are they trying to tell me something?

I've just seen a dentist, having a fight with a manicurist. They were going at it tooth and nail.

I turned the corner and there was another fight, this time between a blacksmith and a hairdresser. Honestly, hammer and tong didn't come into it.

A fresh wave of redundancies has just been announced at the Newquay Surfing Company.

I'm pro-anti: I support my mother's sister.

The new Chelsea manager has been seen wearing blue overalls and carrying a mop and bucket. Early word is they've hired another caretaker.

I went to Berlin and bet two hundred thousand Euros at roulette. The croupier said, are you sure about this? I said, you can bet your bottom Deutschmark I am.

There was this film on last night which finished with a chicken being hit over the head with a frying pan. I thought, great story but what a stupid hen-ding.

It may be a small world. But I still wouldn't fancy paying for it carpeted.

I went to bed and woke up in a parallel universe. I couldn't believe it. In actual fact, I was beside myself.

That film and its remake, where the occupants of an Antarctica research station discover an alien in a block of ice and then fight to stay alive as it consumes them one by one, they've finally completed the trilogy. Critics say it's the best Thing since sliced bread.

I watched Pulp Fiction last night. It was all about some bloke, pretending he owned a paper mill.

That lorry load of turf I stole from the garden centre. Someone grassed me up.

I saw these pieces of fruit on their way into a meeting. I thought, whey hey, conference pairs.

That mass murderer, the one who was going round, clobbering victims with a toastie machine, Mel Gibson is starring in the lead role of a film about his life. It's going to be called, Tefal Weapon.

I live in a counsel house. My home has been taken over by the Samaritans.

There was this notice in the surgery, offering free MOT tests to anyone aged fifty or over. I said to the receptionist, can I book a Renault Megane in for Friday morning?

I couldn't remember where I'd put my boomerang. Then it came back to me.

A glass of water and a test tube of blood entered the pub quiz: the water won. As they always say, blood is thicker than water.

I've just ended my business interest in the fortune telling consultancy. There was no prophet in it.

Last will and testament: it's a dead giveaway.

I took my wife shopping to an artificial limb store. It cost me an arm and a leg.

My wife's a material girl. She's part cotton, part velour.

I followed a sign saying, diverted traffic. When I got there, it was this bloke called Ted, pulling on a diver suit.

When I applied for a credit card, I was asked for my mother's maiden name. I told them it was Voyage.

I used to go out with this letter of the alphabet. Then we broke up. But now we're back together again, me and the X.

Every time someone asks me a question, I reply with a series grammatically related words. I can't help it: it's just a phrase I'm going through.

I started work at McDonalds. But I couldn't cut the mustard.

My hard-up, short-sighted girlfriend took her jewellery to a pawn shop. She arrived home in a naughty nurse's outfit, brandishing a whip.

I said, doctor, I can't stop thinking I'm a puss-filled bleb on a bottle of orange pop. He said, you're such a Fanta cyst.

I offered these crisps a lift. They turned me down: they were Walkers.

That speed limit marker factory near me, it's supposed to be opening up again. But there are no signs yet.

I was boarding this flight when I spotted an old mate of mine a few seats ahead. Next thing, I was in handcuffs and on my way to the police station. All I did was shout, Hi Jack!

All the tools in the box were crying their eyes out. Except, of course, for the coping saw.

I enrolled my new puppy for training classes, but we were the only ones who turned up. Word is the rest were wagging it.

Breaking wind: what a gas.

I was in the bookies, giving medical assistance, while watching the 3.30 from Kempton Park. I was arrested for aiding and abetting.

The dispute at the match factory has finally been resolved after workers accepted strike action could only succeed in inflaming the situation.

I told my workmate I was sick of eating the apples the wife puts in my lunchbox. He told me to grow a pear.

That new Rocky film was a bit disappointing: it was all about a packet of Fox's chocolate biscuits.

I'm doing a bit of market research: there's a decent one in Barnsley and another in Bakewell.

I saw this bloke leg an electric pylon up. He was obviously on a power trip.

Rats: what they don't gnaw isn't worth gnawing.

I hitched a lift on board the Millennium Falcon and landed in a star system filled with exotic birds. It was a parrot-lel universe.

When Einstein revealed his theory of relatively, I thought, it's about time.

I got locked in this container and shipped off to Singapore. Honestly, it was a freight worse than death.

My wife threatened to leave me if I didn't re-decorate the house. I said, that's emulsional blackmail.

The wife won, of course, and left a note next morning saying, don't forget pasting table. So I rang Sting up, asked him how much for the table, and paid him twenty quid on my card.

I was just about to tap the ball into an open goal when I fell down a twenty foot hole. I was sent off for descent.

That documentary about OCD, I watched it a hundred and eighty-three times.

I watched The Exorcist and it scared me half to death. I'm just a bit worried what will happen if I watch it again.

First night in my new house and I didn't sleep a wink for this infernal ticking noise. I found out next morning it was the neighbourhood watch.

The book I'm reading about boxers' training routines: I've skipped a couple of chapters.

I fell out with a refrigeration engineer. But now it's all water under the fridge.

Vicars: they never altar.

I had a spell in prison. I made up this ditty and turned my cellmate into a rabbit.

My friend owns a golf course. He also looks like a bird of prey. His name is Glenn Eagles.

I took my golfing socks back to the shop. There was a hole in one.

I didn't half get my hopes up when my friend said he could get me on at the Action Man factory. As it turned out, he was just toying with me.

I've always been a pessimist. When I went for a blood test, I was B negative.

There was this horrendous coughing and spluttering noise coming from the sky. It was an ill wind.

Some bloke called John Logie invented televisions. A little Baird told me.

I said, doctor, I've got a blister-like swelling on my lip that won't stop shivering. He said, relax, it's just a cold sore.

Two beaches got married. But it didn't last. Now they're both shingle again.

It may be a long shot but, when I grow up, I'd like to be a sniper.

My personal trainer's job: it's not working out.

I went to the Cannes Film Festival. I got seated between tins of spaghetti hoops and baked beans.

13425627R00073

Printed in Great Britain
by Amazon.co.uk, Ltd.,
Marston Gate.